THROUGH A RED PLACE

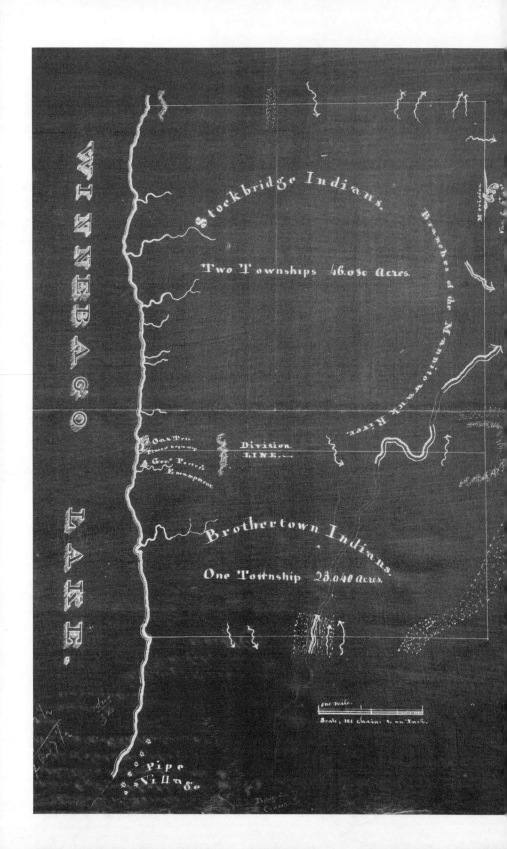

WINNEBAGO LAKE.

Stockbridge Indians.

Two Townships 46.080 Acres.

Branches of the Manitowock River.

Meridian

Oak Tree
Trade begaway

Division
LINE.

Gree Pottei
Encampment

Brothertown Indians.

One Township 23.040 Acres.

one mile.

Scale, 40 chains to an Inch.

Pipe
Village

THROUGH
a RED PLACE

Rebecca Pelky

perugia
PRESS

FLORENCE, MASSACHUSETTS
2021

Perugia Press extends deeply felt thanks to the many individuals whose generosity made the publication of *Through a Red Place* possible. Perugia Press is a tax-exempt, nonprofit 501(c)(3) corporation publishing first and second books of poetry by women. To make a tax-deductible donation, please contact us directly or visit our website.

Book design by Jeff Potter, Rebecca Pelky, and Rebecca Olander

Author photograph by Karen Pelky

Cover art: "Three Sisters," 2020, 16" × 20" (acrylic on stretched canvas), by Kristin Emilyta, a self-taught acrylic artist from Norwich, CT. Her great-great-grandfather was the famed Mohegan Chief Matahga aka Burrill Fielding (1862–1952). Her grandmother was beloved Mohegan elder Margaret LaVigne (1930–2010). Her mother, Laura LaVigne, spent her career working for the Mohegan Cultural & Community Programs Department. Kristin carries on that family legacy of service to her community with her art. She paints professionally and shares her gift with her Mohegan community and the general public by teaching art classes. Her work has been exhibited at the Mohegan Cultural Preservation Center and the Wadsworth Atheneum Museum of Art in Hartford, CT.

Artist contact: Etsy.com/shop/ArtByKristinEmilyta; Instagram: @emilyta_art

Library of Congress Cataloging-in-Publication Data

Names: Pelky, Rebecca, author.
Title: Through a red place / Rebecca Pelky.
Description: Florence, MA : Perugia Press, 2021. | Some poems are written in both English and Mohegan. | Summary: "Rebecca Pelky's story-in-poems assembles the author's research into her Native and non-Native heritage in the land now known as Wisconsin. Through the poet's ancestors-and documented through text and image-this book relates narratives of people who converged on and impacted this space in myriad ways. Written in English and Mohegan, Through a Red Place reshapes itself from page to page, asking what it means to navigate place as both colonizer and colonized. These poems seek the interior and exterior lives of beloved people and places, interacting with archives and visuals to illustrate that what is past continually interrupts and reinscribes itself upon the present. This collection embodies a refusal to go missing despite what's buried, erased, or built over, much like the ancient mound now covered by an ammunition plant. An inventive collage of geography, history, myth, translation, lineage, erasure, journalism, and photography, Through a Red Place builds a map between distances and lost stories to unearth and honor the past"-- Provided by publisher.
Identifiers: LCCN 2021033147 | ISBN 9780997807653 (paperback)
Subjects: LCGFT: Poetry. | Prose poems.
Classification: LCC PS3616.E366 T48 2021 | DDC 811/.6--dc23
LC record available at https://lccn.loc.gov/2021033147

Perugia Press
PO Box 60364
Florence, MA 01062
editor@perugiapress.org
perugiapress.org

For all the ancestors

Yo mutah mutu nutah, wipi kutah.
This heart is not mine, but yours.
~Sachem Uncas

Nuwacônumumun yoht wáci napukak.
We keep a fire for the dead.

CONTENTS

WIKSAPÁKAT WIYON

Kucuhshun katumuw, qá wiksapákahk.
Muhtuqash wiksapákahks wuyôcánumunáwôwh.

Kahôkak piyôk nanumayo.
Áhsituk kupat wasapáyuw.

Iyo kuquskacámun tayôsqônuk.
Mus numic wici kahak wiksapákahk.

MAPLE SUGAR MOON

The year begins in sweetness.
The maple trees open.

The geese come north.
Ice dies on the river.

Now we are crossing the bridge.
I will eat that syrup with you.

EFFIGY

Let's begin
with a snake, sunk into the plateau
or raised up from the creek through the meteor
crater, ages ago, they say, when reptiles still had legs.
If I were a snake, I'd point my coils too, toward solstice—
sunrise on the shortest day, a warning. A deep curve
of grassy scale for summer, another for fall.
A spiral of tail I'd follow inward until what I know
shifts and sloughs off my skin.

> Fidelia wrote in her diary, *Yesterday,*
> *I saw in the river a snake with a fish in her mouth.*
> *The fish was handsome. The snake was ugly.*
> We never were serpent people.

I lay a palm on the snake's nose. The earth
is warm underneath. I am warm, underneath,
the pulse in my palm pressed to a forked tongue
as the wind picks up, hissing through the trees.

❁

Or, let's begin with what we can only imagine
as a fort, because all we can see in shared walls
is war, not what they might have upheld, not
that the bones of ancestors built
into infrastructure might be less guards
than counsel. Rock mounds pilfered
because all we dream worth saving
in the ground is gold. Here X marks
the solstice—the sun, a winter treasure—

THE SERPENT MOUND, SERPENT MOUND PARK, NEAR
LOUDEN, ADAMS COUNTY, OHIO.

or my great-great grandmother's name,
the long and short of her years as two crossed lines
on smudged parchment. I know so little
of her, besides this. I know so little

of these people, except that they tracked
the sky, harvested plants we clear as weeds,
worked copper and earth and stone to effigies,
kept their dead at their doorsteps,
and built a fort with 83 doors.

✻

Now let's end
at the Wisconsin State Capitol
and its one grand door, where
they dug the nearby mounds for fill,
tamped down to foundations
to build their own little hill, the bones
of a people shouldering someone
else's state, shattered turtle shells.

These are not your council.

And looking down over it all, a globe
clutched in one palm, a girl done up
in gold, a woman named Wisconsin.

So with that we're back to a snake, a river
the Miami called Meskonsing, we're back
to the truth of a name she never knew
she bore: Wisconsin. It lies
in a red place.

CROSSING THE MIDWEST ON
THE WINTER SOLSTICE

On the shortest day, I leave and arrive in darkness.
Sunrise, sunset, reds in the windshield, the rearview.
In the short light, billboards for Jesus plod by, poems
that grow, line by line, along fenced fields of dirty snow.

Their forced-rhymed, hand-paint screams we all need guns
to keep the bad guys at bay. Hawks in the leafless trees,
hawk after hawk, until it's the same hawk again, the same
gray branches. I've passed this way so many times before.

But this is my ceremony, this long drive north, this span
of land and daylight. These are the lines that cross,
that bind me again and again to this place, until
it's the once-plains that cross me, generations in the making.

NUNIHTUHTO MOHIKS, NUQUT

Nutakis kowák wôpáks
kuski máy—nuqut,
nupáw, nisôsk—aqi
nutakis máy:

sôwanayo, máqamtunayo, wômiyo,
nanummayo, wôpanayo, kuhkuhqi.

Nutakis ayômi nahak:
máy nisôskut.
Cahsuwak kowák wôpáks
apuwak ayômi nahak.

LEARNING MOHEGAN #1

I count the white pines
along the road—one,
five, seven—like I count
the ways I can go:

south, west, down,
north, east, up.

I count within myself:
the seventh direction.
There are many more
white pines inside me.

KOPAYÁHS WIYON

Kihtamsh sisikocik kopayáhsak;
kutomák i sasôkapámuk

yôcánuk. Cáqan kutus
putaman kopayáhsak?

Nutôcimohkawô ihtôqat. Ôtay, kihtôqat
mus kupahkacihto wici macuhsh kupat.

PEEPING FROG MOON

Listen to the peeping frogs;
they sing the sassafras tree

into bloom. What are you doing
when you hear them?

I am telling a story. Then, your story
will end only with the last ice.

MIXED BLOOD

Somewhere in the white spaces
between generations, the stories
got lost. I knew the word Indian
like an echo—on a screen,
on a page, but never in a body,
never a warm body filled with song.
My father—lost to alcohol and Vietnam,
to a world that wouldn't let him love
a man—was the first true story I knew.

Lost to my father, I clung to a worn photo
of my grandmother as a young woman—
gray skin, gray clapboard house, gray sky,
gray clothes, gray dirt in a gray dust bowl
in Wisconsin. Close to my face, her eyes,
tipped down at the outside, were mine.
I clung to the corners of those eyes.

Mixed blood, I kept moving, kept asking,
Do I fit here? Or here? Or here? Not quite,
never quite. So finally, tired, I planted my feet
and started pulling instead—gathering, collecting,
hauling everything into my body, my Indian-
on-the-inside body. I held it all. I swallowed
stories, breathed in Mohegan, tugged and
tugged on the line that brought me down
400 years to Lucy Cochegan and Mourning
Dove and Hannah Ashbow, and though I never saw
their eyes, I knew. I knew they were mine.

ACNESTIS 1

My mother and I walk back and forth down crooked lines of
intermittent headstones, some so covered by grass that they can't
be read. It's sad, we say to each other, that no one comes. No one
kicks back the clippings or tears away what's overgrown. It's hot
for June in northern Wisconsin and moving keeps the mosquitos
at bay when the breeze dies. We're in a place once called Potter's
Field, for those too poor to pay for burial, or who have no one to take
care of them in death. The woman in the office, who I go to when
our search is fruitless, tells me in a hush that they don't call it that
anymore. She says some sixty percent of the graves are unmarked,
that all the space I walked on like lawn was gridded full. She has
a map. Dug up from a back room, rolled into a tube and flaking
like dead skin, the transparent paper displays a crowded quilt of
names. There was an outbreak, she says, lots of people at the same
time. When I ask if they'd ever digitize the map, she brushes this
off with a why-bother shrug. Nobody much comes looking. I click
pictures on my phone nonetheless. Back in Section T, I know where
I'm going. I know from the faded script on the map, from the names
on the headstones next to them, the ones kitty-corner. I judge the
length of lawn between bodies with my own. They're here, I tell
my mother, unmarked. She doesn't understand, but it's important
that I stand on the exact spot, as if I have to align myself just right,
as if I'm waiting for family to puzzle into place, a cat's cradle of
stretched string that will snap itself to a grid, the perfect tension
telling me that this is finally where I fit.

LUCY

Nikôni nunonôk,
apuw yo qut nuskansh, qut mutu
wipi nuskansh. Cáhak apuw?
Tatô. Apuw
aqu Eeyamquittoowauconnuck.

LUCY

First mother,
now just bones, but not
just bones. I don't know
where she is. Somewhere
under Brothertown.

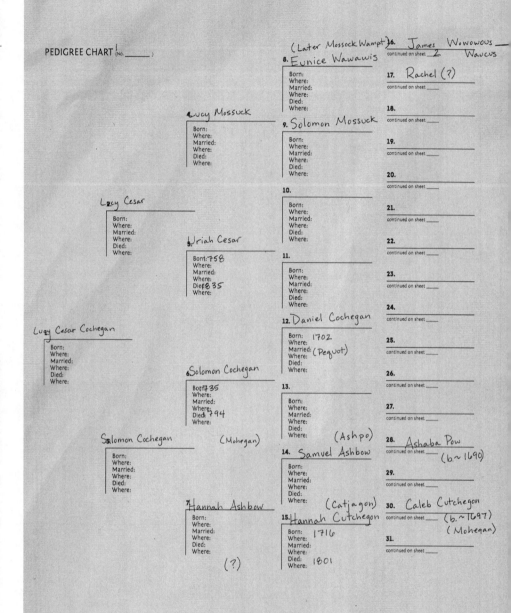

Lucy Cesar Cochegan
Born:
Where:
Married:
Where:
Died:
Where:

Lucy Cesar
Born:
Where:
Married:
Where:
Died:
Where:

Solomon Cochegan
Born:
Where:
Married:
Where:
Died:
Where:

4. Lucy Mossuck
Born:
Where:
Married:
Where:
Died:
Where:

5. Uriah Cesar
Born: 758
Where:
Married:
Where:
Died: 835
Where:

6. Solomon Cochegan
Born: 735
Where:
Married:
Where: 794
Died:
Where:

7. Hannah Ashbow
Born:
Where:
Married:
Where:
Died:
Where:
(?)

(Later Mossock Wampt.)
8. Eunice Wawawis
Born:
Where:
Married:
Where:
Died:
Where:

9. Solomon Mossuck
Born:
Where:
Married:
Where:
Died:
Where:

10.
Born:
Where:
Married:
Where:
Died:
Where:

11.
Born:
Where:
Married:
Where:
Died:
Where:

12. Daniel Cochegan
Born: 1702
Where:
Married: (Pequot)
Where:
Died:
Where:

13.
Born:
Where:
Married:
Where:
Died:
Where: (Ashpo)

(Mohegan)
14. Samuel Ashbow
Born:
Where:
Married:
Where:
Died:
Where: (Catjagon)

15. Hannah Cutchegon
Born: 1716
Where:
Married:
Where:
Died: 1801
Where:

16. James Wowowous
continued on sheet 2 Waucus

17. Rachel (?)
continued on sheet ____

18.
continued on sheet ____

19.
continued on sheet ____

20.
continued on sheet ____

21.
continued on sheet ____

22.
continued on sheet ____

23.
continued on sheet ____

24.
continued on sheet ____

25.
continued on sheet ____

26.
continued on sheet ____

27.
continued on sheet ____

28. Ashaba Pow
continued on sheet ____ (b. ~ 1690)

29.
continued on sheet ____

30. Caleb Cutchegon
continued on sheet ____ (b. ~ 1697)
(Mohegan)

31.
continued on sheet ____

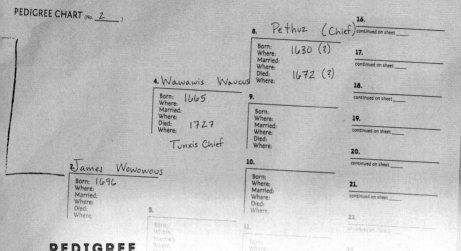

8. Pethuz (Chief) continued on sheet ____

Born:
Where: 1630 (?)
Married:
Where:
Died: 1672 (?)
Where:

4. Wawawis Wavcus
Born: 1665
Where:
Married:
Where:
Died: 1727
Where:

Tunxis Chief

16.

17. continued on sheet ____

18. continued on sheet ____

9.
Born:
Where:
Married:
Where:
Died:
Where:

19. continued on sheet ____

20. continued on sheet ____

2. James Wowowous
Born: 1696
Where:
Married:
Where:
Died:
Where:

10.
Born:
Where:
Married:
Where:
Died:
Where:

21. continued on sheet ____

1.
Born:
Where:
Married:
Where:
Died:
Where:

PEDIGREE

There's something skeletal about it.
Though we call them trees, they seem
unfleshed, like they'll never be more
than dug-up bones laid out and labeled
on bleached tables.

Pedigree:

It needs thicker sinew, the raw
red meat of stories to flesh
the bony processes of names and
dates. It needs the scarred skin
of history, even if just to peel it away.

Pedigree,

as if bred, like it all comes down
to me, and now I'm at some show,
balancing on bones stacked end
to end, like I'm here to score my color
and form, strip back my imperfect
skin to read what's written in my blood.

COCHEGAN

When written: Coeghegan, Cutchegum, Skeegan.
The names of my Mohegan ancestors.
The name of a boulder, dropped
on what would be Connecticut,
where my family once met.

The name of a bull, owned
by Colt, Samuel C., on an index
of bulls with names like Indiana Chief
or Chesapeake Chief or Cattaraugus Chief.
These butchered names, all, such strange honors.

THE MONTH OF THREE MILKINGS

May has no more time for witches.
In Wisconsin, Walpurgisnacht

makes way for dairy farmers
who get up too early for late-night

revels with old Germanic gods. In 2017
a Wisconsin Holstein broke the world

record for milk production. Her owner
says My Gold was born for greatness.

WÔMÔSUM

~Ihtôqat muskamôn

Nunáwô nahak
pipinacucôhqôkanuk. Nuputawô nahak
pupiqáwôkanuk. Awán na

sqá? Cahsuwak quniqák
apuwak wukupáy? Cahshinsh punitôkansh
suhkuhkanum? Cáqansh manotásh

nákum mus ayakumun? Nám
piwáhcuks upihsháwônsh. Wáhtôw
másqák sipo. Wahakáh náwáw

pipinacucôhqôkanuk. Putawáw wahakáh iwát,
*Katawi-kuwômôyi
mucimi.*

LOVE ME

~ A found poem

I see myself
in the mirror. I hear myself
in the music. Who is that

woman? How many deer are there
in her forest? How many knives
can she throw? What baskets

will she paint? She sees that
the flowers are little. She knows
the river is red. She sees herself

in the mirror. She hears herself say,
You are going to love me
forever.

OFFERING

I could bury my head
here, in the sand, salt it,
jar it, spend days drowning

and breathing. I could pluck
each finger and let it flutter
to the tide. I love me. I love me
not. I could build a fortress,

moat the bounding main,
replace my eyes with sea glass
and tint my life vermillion.

I could trade my tongue
for leaves of leathered kelp
and learn to speak
in seaweed and brine.

LOST

When Patience disappeared
it was still winter, but late,
so maybe it was shrugged off
as thin ice, until August,
when she still wasn't found.

I wonder what spawned
such late concern. After all,
history tells us,
These things happen
to Indian girls. Patience

wasn't my kin, not in the thick
blood way, but more like how
we say Nation and it means
something closer to cousins,
the kind you meet dredging

the same thawed lake
when you're all searching
for different lost things.
Is it enough, if all we have
together is trauma?

Even when homecoming
doesn't feel much like home
in a bare room full of strangers,
here we all are again, all drawn
back to the same place, as if

to be seen, as if to say, *I am*
not missing. Not yet. Not today.

LOST.

PATIENCE FOWLER, a girl of the
Brothertown tribe of Indians, left her
mother's residence at Deansburgh on the
East side of the Winnebago Lake, on the
10th day of last March. She is supposed to
have wandered in a South East direction.
She will be 12 years old the 4th of next Sept.
had a scar near the top of her head, where
their was no hair; had black hair, black eyes
and a fair complexion; spoke no language but
the English when she left home. Any infor-
mation concerning such a girl given at this
Office or communicated to Patience Fowler,
Deansburgh, Grand Cakalin P. O., will be
most gratefully received, and the person giving it amply rewarded.
Green Bay Aug. 9, 1835.

WUTÁHUM WIYON

Ôkowi mô kuwutahki muhtáwiyush wiyonak,
wipi iyo kuputuki.

Nikoni kipunumuwôk mihkáyuw wiyámoyak,
wipi kupáhtomun wiksapákatôk. Yotay,

qucimôtamsh upihsháwansh muhtuquk wuci náhtiyá.
Yotay, nutáh wiksapákat, ayaksak pon kisukuk.

HEARTBERRY MOON

You lived away for many months,
but now you have come back.

The first picking is strong medicine,
but what we wait for is sweet. Here,

smell the dogwood blossoms.
Here, my sweetheart, put the stars in the sky.

MUCÁQ

Mic musqáyuw áyakunuk mutonuk,
pitkôsonsh musqáyuw mômôci wutunuk
aqi wahakayash wuci wiwáhcumunsh,

aqi wahakayash wuci piyámáqak sawáyush,
aqi nákatuk kisi
mô mohwáwak sqák.

Ôkutak awán kámotuk piyô yotay.
Ôkutak awán kámotuk piyô yotay.
Ôkutak awán kámotuk piyô yotay.

Cahsuwak sqák mus kumotuwak?
Cahsuwak wuci nutônihsunônak
mus "náyuwáyuwak?"

Yotay wuyam másqák kumuskam.

GONE

A red hand painted on a mouth,
red dresses stir in the wind, empty
like corn husks,

like fish scales are empty,
like what's left after
the women were consumed.

Here comes another thief.
Here comes another thief.
Here comes another thief.

How many women will they take?
How many of our daughters
will "wander off?"

You'll find the red paint here.

PARRISH

Men arranged this
with other men,
sent Indian girls away
to learn good godly ways.

And the women learned
things they already knew:
how to clean, how to cook,
how to serve. For their teachers
were devout and only wanted
to save the Indians.

It all reads so agreeable
from the white
pages, a good Christian
doing God's work. Indians
eager to embrace
an escape from heathen ways,

slavery, starvation.
I wonder what's unsaid.
If they were traded. After all,
what are two daughters
in exchange for good graces?

Did Parrish see them
in their blankets as quiescent,
the silence of devotion rather
than the paralysis of terror?

Did he imagine them chrysalises
that, only by his intervention,

would become worthy, if fragile?
Did he think he was raising
butterflies, only to clip their wings?

8th. A hard frost. This morning, set out for Brothertown, having the Chief's horse to ride, with one
of their principal men for a guide. We travelled
through a most fertile country, over logs, and through
bushes, at the rate of about a mile, and sometimes
two, in an hour. Arrived at Brothertown in the evening, and were treated with all the kindness we could
ask. Having comfortably lodged here one night, the
next day we set out for Fort Schuyler, being still ac-
commodated with horses and a guide. The roads
were beyond description, bad; but we were favoured
to reach Fort Schuyler, in the evening,—having pre-
viously agreed to meet our family of female Indians
at this place.

10th. This morning our Indian girls came, each
one accompanied by her parent or guardian. The
business of parting was conducted with great serious-
ness, for the Indians delivered their children to us
with the utmost confidence and quietude: which
brought over my mind a considerable weight of concern and care, that nothing on my part, might ob-
struct this great and important work. The girls ma-
nifested much stillness and composure, at taking leave
of their parents, to go a long journey, with perfect
strangers, to reside in a distant land. So we went to
the Mohawk river, and they stepped into the boat,
wrapped their faces in their blankets, and I do not remember that they uttered a word. We now had to
pass down this river about one hundred miles, but
got on very well the first day's voyage.

In the course of a few days, we had them stationed
at the Friends' houses, who were willing to take
charge of them, and instruct them in the business of
housewifery. Two of the girls were placed with Na-
than Coope and son;—one, with a woman Friend,
who had a concern to take charge of one of the Indians;—one was placed with the family of William
Jackson, and the remaining two with Isaac Jackson.
At my taking leave of them, they wept considerably;

MOHICAN

~A Last of the Mohicans *found poem*

Strives ~~Bolingbroke~~ [Cooper] to be as great as we?
Greater he shall not be... ~ Shakespeare, Richard II

Here I am.
I am glad.
I am thankful that, though
I am no scholar, I am not
a prejudiced man.
I am certain.
I am genuine.
I am willing.

I am a blazed pine.
I am outlying.
I am journeying.
I am on the hilltop and must
go down into the valley;
I am as ready to do one as the other,
for I am on ground
that I have often traveled.

I am sorry. I am not sorry
I am very happy.
I am sure. I am sure
I am ready.
I am rejoiced.
I am suffered.
I am resolved.

I am a man.
I am a man.
I am a man.
Am I, then so
very revolting?

I am your prisoner.
I am your prisoner.
I am stripped.
I am torn.

I am not alone.
I am not stone.
I am not the last.

Stockbridge - Wis.

Record of Graduates and Returned Students.

U. S. INDIAN SCHOOL, CARLISLE, PA.

NAME *Wm. J. Moon* May 24th 1910.

1. Are you married and if so to whom? *I am married to a Cherokee Custa Indian.*

2. What is your present address? *Ashkosh*

3. Did you attend or graduate from any other schools after leaving Carlisle? *No* Give names of schools and dates if possible

MOHICAN

4. What is your present occupation? *is cement work. My present occupation*

5. Tell something of your present home: *have built this Spring and it is worth $1000. I have a new home*

6. What property in the way of land, stock, buildings or money do you have? *I have one house and a lot.*

7. Have you been in the Indian Service? In what positions? How long in each? *No*

JULY

Sell the lambs and save the deer;
these are the dog days, the lion

and the crab days. These are
the freedom days and firework

nights, shark week, and
The Month of the Most

Precious Blood of Jesus.

BIRD MOUND FACING DEVIL'S LAKE

The lake was here long before the Devil
held sway in Wisconsin (and by that name,
I mean where the river runs through
the red place). Devil's Lake isn't
its first name, but settlers heard Spirit Lake,
Da-wa-kah-char-gra, and read evil
in the earth-bound sacred. A lake
without inlet or outlet could only be bound
to the underworld, and we know what that means.

The story is, Devil's Lake was part of the river once,
until glaciers came and went, leaving
moraines in the gorges and forcing the river
to bow around Baraboo's Hills.
There's something sad about that, like the lake
is a child, caged and curled in a ball, and the river
a mother, chewing through a wall of bedrock to return.

❋

Bird Mound could be a swallow-tailed kite
about to take off from the shoreline.
Their range, before we came, once
included the borders of Wisconsin
(and by that name, I mean the state
that won't recognize my tribe, though we
came here before the land was cut on dotted lines).

Or maybe Bird Mound is really Thunderbird,
about to be dragged into the lake
by Mishibijiw, the Underwater Panther.

It's a story I heard once, about this place.

There's an Underwater Panther Mound
across the lake, maybe squaring up. Mishibijiw
will drown you, they say. Or maybe Thunderbird
has finally climbed out onto the shore, and now
he rests. Maybe one day he'll wake up,
and the cliffs of Wisconsin will shudder again
with his voice (and by his voice, I mean
wámi kukikátohkámun).

Right now, it's tourist season in Wisconsin
(and by that name I mean the state whose motto is
"Forward"). A slow wave of people come and go,
giving little attention to Bird Mound
blooming with prairie plants. The water
draws them, and after all, Devil's Lake is just
a name, and these vacationers have forgotten
to fear spirits, at least in daylight.

At some point enough people cut across
one wing so that it could be broken,
a rutted trail bisecting a small hill prairie.
Maybe it felt like an echo of great adventure
for children raised to set themselves as kings
of every hill, but not to see every hill as a king.

❀

Hummingbirds dart over Bird Mound,
between the purple spiderwort, maybe
looking for something more to their liking,
or maybe, from the sky, they see themselves
writ large among the prairie plants. Who doesn't
want to be closer to their gods?

❀

When a friend posts pictures on Facebook
of camping and hiking around Devil's Lake,
there are no photos of the mounds,
which isn't surprising.

If you picked up the guidebook, they'd be tucked in
the far back. But in one lake shot, from a rise above,
I can see where Bird Mound should be, behind the trees,
next to the picnic shelter and the beach. People go,
or maybe arrive, wading in. From this perspective,
it might look like Bird Mound was about to fly,
to settle its feathers of switchgrass and prairie
dropseed before pushing off over the green
water of Spirit Lake.

35

SIR:

I hereby make application for such share as may be due me of the fund appropriated by the Act of Congress, approved June 30, 1906, in accordance with the decrees of the Court of Claims of May 18, 1905, and May 28, 1906, in favor of the Eastern Cherokees. The evidence of identity is herewith subjoined.

NOTE: Answers to all questions should be short, but complete. If you can not answer, so state.

1. State full name—

    English name: Aaron Roberts

    Indian name: unknown

2. Residence and post office: 55 Custer St Oshkosh Wis

3. County: Winebago

4. State: Wisconsin

5. How old are you? 58 years Born 1848

6. Where were you born? Orany Co. Indiana

7. Are you married? Yes

8. Name and age of wife or husband: Rachel Roberts

9. To what tribe of Indians does he or she belong? Brother town

10. Name all your children who were living on May 28, 1906, giving their ages:

NAME.	AGE.	BORN.
(1) Anna Butts	46 year	unknown
(2) Nelbert Roberts	24 "	May 25, 1877
(3) Authur Robert	28 "	June 2 1779
(4) Sarah A. Waldow	unknown	unknown
(5) Burrel Boller	15 years	1892
(6) Churless Boller	13 "	1896
Robert Boller	13 "	1894

11. Give names of your father and mother, and your mother's name before marriage:

    Father—English name: Ishmael Roberts

    Indian name: unknown

    Mother—English name: Delaney Roberts

    Indian name: unknown

    Maiden name: Delany Revels

12. Where were they born?

    Father: N Carolina

    Mother: Georgia

CEMETERY ETIQUETTE

I set my feet in the dirt beneath headstone after headstone, hot August marble in the sharp cut grass. Next to one cemetery, a dozen yards away, a farmer works in a metal barn. Near another, a power plant hums, and I wonder how it is to sleep here. With my toes hooked into grave dirt, I first ask for forgiveness. I should've brought something, a small gift, but because it's all that I have, I sit and tell the stones my stories. I tell Delana Revels what I'm reading, because her pedestal is topped by an open book. I give her some lines I remember, and I hope she was a reader, like me. I hope she scribbled poetry into notebooks. This stone is almost all I know about her. I ask too, about her son Aaron, and who knows, maybe the doe that wandered past bleating for her fawn was a kind of answer. I wish I could ask her about Ishmael, her husband, whose grave is two states distant. They met when their families, Black and Cherokee, fled north from North Carolina. Sons and daughters married in the stuttered migrations across new states. Her son is forty-five miles away, and I wonder if he, who survived the Civil War, 29th Colored Infantry, wasn't allowed to be buried in such places. I don't know if this is true. An aunt told me once that he played the fife, which looks an awful lot like the recorders we played in grade school, so I tell Delana about this too. I think that with these stories, I'm a kind of link between their distance. Or maybe I'm a story they're still telling.

KÔKCI KON

Awán ki, nunánu Kôkci Kon?
Mô kuputaqi aqu konak wôpis'hutut,
wuták ahshay wôpisuk.
Mô kuputaqi aqu wánuksak.

Wipi kôcuci kuwáhush.
Ki mô kutay wutônihsuwôwah. Ki, winay,
mô wáskinut. Yôwatuk mô kupumshá
akômuk Nupsapáqash Makáks.

Páhki kuskisuquash ayuwak nuskisuqashuk.
Ki mô kutay ohsuhsuwôwah.
Ki kutay aqi ni.

GREAT SNOW

Who are you, Grandmother Cochegan?
You have been hidden under white snow,
behind white paper.
You have been buried under white people.

But I know you, a little.
You were a daughter. You were a young woman
and an old woman. You walked far
across the Great Lakes.

Maybe your eyes are my eyes.
You were a granddaughter.
You were me.

I NEVER WAS A TRAIN-TRACK GIRL

Though I am bound,
I won't ask for your help.
I'm not silent

film, not lipstick, not the girl
in King Kong's fist.
I'd break thumbs

to shrug off my ropes. In the end,
if we kissed, your mouth
would taste like the desert

outside Winslow, Arizona,
where a meteor left a hole
two and a half miles wide.

AUGUST

Though I am thirsty, I will not tell you.
I'd rather lick the salt from my palms,

let it pucker beneath my tongue,
let it taint the words I'll spit. In drought,

my body is a saltwater roadmap.
Oh, how these almost-stars have marked me.

THE WHITES OF NEW YORK

~A Last of the Mohicans *found poem*

What have you left to us of land, what have you left of game,
What have you brought but evil, and curses since you came?
How have you paid us for our game? how paid us for our land?
By a book, *to save our souls from the sins* you brought in your
other hand. ~E. Pauline Johnson (Mohawk)

The white men are coming!
The white men are coming!
A white man leads the way.
A good deal sullied, the white man, armed
(the gift of the white man lies in his arms).
The white man, judging.
Whites, the most dangerous of all.
The white man loosened his knife.

The white man, observing the Indian:
I am genuine white, a white man
who has no taint, who has the full blood
of the whites. My judgment is greater.
I am a man of white blood, and being a white-
skin, I will not deny my nature.

But you are just a man.

The white man, shaking his head.
What to do with these dumb creatures,
muttered the white man (it is rare
for a white voice to pitch itself properly).
Go, said the white man.
The white man prevailed. White blood,
blood of the whites. It is not to be denied
that evil has been mainly done
by men with white skins.

✳

White fathers.
        White usurpers.

            White flag.

                Christian whites.
White veins.
        White eyes.

                White hunter.
White uniforms.

      White warrior.

        White quarrel.

                White cunning.

      White experience.

The notions of white men.

      Fabrication of the whites.

              Execution, the white men.

CÁQANSH WÁSQAKS

Mus kutuyush itôqat.
Kuwáhto mô pásawucôn yotay
qá nákayucôn? Nuwahô skitôp
mô áyasunuqiyôn i ahsit.

Mô iwá nuquhshuqun.
Mô iwá, *Wikun wisuyôn.*

Áhsituk, mô nutôkosu,
mô nunatskawáw piyámáq
mohak. Mô nukawi.
Yôpôwi, mô nutohki.

Mô nutiwá, *Kutáhqôhtamôsh.*
Nunôhtuyô takôk puquiyuk.

SHARP THINGS

I'll tell you the story.
You know that I was brought here,
and left? I know the person
that led me to the river.

He said that we scared him.
He said, *It's good that I hurt you.*

At the river, I prayed,
I chased the fish,
that I might eat it. I slept.
In the morning, I woke up.

I said, *I forgive you.*
I showed him the hatchet in the ashes.

MY MOTHER TOLD ME THIS STORY:

When I was carrying you, and I was about seven months along, your Grandma Pelky knew I was afraid of delivering. So she took me down to the schoolyard, when all the kids were out for play time, and she said,

> *Now look at all them kids. All their mothers are still alive and delivered each one of the kids and are all still here. And you will be fine also.*

She wasn't my mother's mother, but my father's, and having delivered seven living boys, she knew. And having no daughters, she gave her story to the youngest wife of her three married sons.

I never met Mable Moon Pelky, the woman in the gray photo. She died of a stroke before I was born. My mother says I look like her, and she worries about my high blood pressure.

When my mother tells this story, my sister has already born two children, and both of us are past the age of having more, so this isn't a story about childbirth, really, but about kinship. It's a cord, they tell me, not just from blood to blood, but from woman to woman.

SEPTEMBER

This is the beginning and the beginning of
the end. At Cahokia the equinox sun is born
from Monks Mound, surrounded by corn, always

corn, a Mexican immigrant, harvested here
all the rich years of Mississippian city life,

and then feeding the settler Midwest. And now,
the sun rises over the St. Louis gateway
and landfill, our new sacred capitalist mound.

MAN MOUNDS

Man Mound is cut off at the knees
by a country road bound by pastures
and barbed wire. It isn't right, but it's perfect
as metaphors go. We say it when we've stolen
someone's power. He was built mid-stride,
so they stilled his momentum

with their own. In white,
they've painted Man Mound's shins
like plaster casts. Or ghosts. As if to recognize,
but not redress. They've limed his feet too,
in a fenced pen, chalk outlines and crime-scene boundaries.
At least he has a crown of ferns on his lobed head,
a quiet wood, a bronze memorial. A note
to respect those who come here to pray.

❋

He has it better than Black Earth Man Mound,
who wears Blue Mounds Street like a loincloth,
and has a house pressed into his chest. It's white,
with shutters and a fenced yard, a two-car garage
in his armpit. Every day people walk down
the stone-lined path of his stomach.

I wonder if the pretty house has a basement,
if they dug out his heart and lined his chest
with mortar and bricks, if they stack Christmas
decorations along his ribs, wash their clothes
in his left lung, play ping-pong in his right.

Another Man is somewhere under the old
Badger Ammunitions Plant. I say under because
according to a survey done in 1983,
no surface evidence exists, although
the locations were mapped in 1910, which means this
Man Mound has been leveled. For the war effort,

Badger Ammunition produced Ball Powder™
first used against the Koreans and then
the Vietnamese. Now the groundwater
causes cancer.

The government shrugged

off clean-up efforts, and offered the toxic land,
the leveled Man, to other federal agencies.

> *The BIA declined to accept any land for the Ho-Chunk Nation,*
> *citing no authority to incur excessive cost...*

> *The Ho-Chunk Nation has been unsuccessful*
> *in changing the BIA's position.*

This land too, then, is cut off at the knees.

BROKEN SKIES AT 5,000 FEET,

the captain said, cloud prairie,
as if the nimbus were plowed
under, barb-wired. Through

post holes, I count dams, ground-
water-ground, broken
in, like panthers waiting

to break out, to become
power, lines drawn in the white-
cloud-dirt, snow pollen, winter tillage.

SONNET FOR THE MOHEGAN LANGUAGE

Without an adjective there is no blue
for bird or sky or water, which is not
to say a colorless world. See the hue
just there of a bird being red as it
builds a nest of twigs and bits of wire
(being gray or being rusty). There is room,
like Cricket laughing himself into fire,
for a bird to blacken sometime soon.
The nest as well, might find its niche
being small and happy while it waits
for eggs and then a family to stretch
the edge for love and size, to make it great.
The Mohegan world isn't static, but flows
prismatic; each of us moves in rainbows.

PUNIPUKAT

Kahôkak piyôk sôwanayo.
Áskot putukunik ahutanishunimukuk,

pukut wuci wutqunsh nuhpuhk'hqashuk.
Nuqáhshap qásqacut.

Punipukat Wiyon piyômush.

FALLING LEAVES

The geese go south.
Pumpkin bread in the oven,

wood smoke in my hair.
I am ready to be cold.

Falling Leaves Moon comes.

REDACTED

Here's what I remember:

Red flowers, beds

    in squares. Yellow. Sepia

        stone paths. Hard

light of day. Everything

    in primaries. Tulips taller

        from the dirt side. This

is just a memory in the overexposed glare

    of some lost context. It makes me uncomfortable,

        the water too far off for sound.

This is where the doors open.

        This is the ground and the thirteenth floor. No smell,

        no thick pollen on my tongue,

        no brush of petals. No touching.

This is where I go. This

    is where I go back to.

        Squinting into a color wheel.

If there were bees and buzzing, they've withered

into the gravel verges. The plane of horizon

tilts and yellow tulips flip,

a thousand balloons drifting.

ACNESTIS 2

I drive the rental car back and forth on the same stretch of curving road, back to the same gravel turn-around. On the porch of a sagging feed store with a Purina logo fading from the blue wooden siding, an old man watches my car come and go again. I'm looking for a gate, a road, a sign to get me to the Revel's family cemetery. I know where it should be, up in the hills, but the trees are a screen, and the rockface the road curves around and the pasture fence snug to the other shoulder don't leave anywhere to park and walk. Between me and where my Cherokee ancestors rest are acres of muddy spring pasture and a herd of Jersey cows. I can see the place on Google Earth. There are no roads, no two-tracks, maybe the faint line of a path, a margin of hedge on the hillside, white dots that might be headstones.

Revels Cemetery

On *findagrave.com* I can pull up pictures of the stones, read a line about lineage. Even here, in the car, far from any town or tower I can do this. But I want my hands in their dirt. I want to trace my fingers down the chiseled stone. I want to leave tobacco, a story, but there's no way in I can find without climbing wire fence and risking both the rancher and the bulls. I think about asking the man at the feed store, but we're alone in the middle of nowhere, and everything I know has taught me that's a bad idea. By now the sun is touching the hilltops, and I'm too deep in Wisconsin's river-lands to be out by dark, so I don't turn in at the gravel dead end. Instead, I give in again to missing what is just out of reach.

LANDMINES

My father's stories got lost. Some died
in jungles with names I don't know,
where so many stories ended up
in unmarked graves. Others, I suspect,
were muttered into empties, then broken
in alleys. I don't know how to piece those.

I heard once he pulled a gun on my uncle
for drug money. What memories I have
are of black eyes that never rested.
I've heard other stories too, but those
are not for you. Some stories are
told without being spoken. Some stories
are between mothers and daughters.

※

There's a wide white space, a gutter
between my father and me—clearcut
jungle, stories planted with landmines.
I find shards that could be excavated,
glued carefully together. I do this
from a safe distance, from musty archives
and computer screens. On Google

Street View, I study a house he lived in,
next to the Premiere Sports Bar,
three houses down from The County
Liquor Store. It's late fall, by the leaves.
There's a man with a blurred face looking into
the camera, passing a plastic Santa and old
jack-o'-lanterns. It could be him, looking back,
and at this thought I'm small, crouching
at a crack in a bedroom door, about to be seen.

☀

That story ends with a blank space,
but old fear still closes in, and I close
the map and all the other tabs.

Some stories belong underground,
unfound. Landmines seethe
like yellowjacket nests. Everyone knows
it's best to leave them alone.

WIYON PÁSUKOKUN

Wiyon mô patupshatôk wunupi,
kuhpayuk mus kuponômun muks.

Nutáh kuhpáyuw.
Aqi cáqan yo máhsunuman?

Mus kunawômun
naspi Acáwôk Wiyon.

NINTH MOON

When the moon has spilled its water,
we will put the wolf in the forest.

My heart is closed.
What is it like when you touch it?

We will see
by the Hunting Moon.

BETWEEN THE LI■ES

~An Andrew Jackson erasure

It gives me pleasure

the removal of the Indians beyond   white
settlements
important tribes have   made   their
last   Congress, and it
will induce
obvious advantages
to the United States,
pecuniary advantages

It will relieve

the Indians
of
power   happiness

progress   lessening their numbers, and
cause
their

certain and
complete execution

Toward the aborigines   no one can indulge a
friendly feeling

I have endeavored to impress upon them my
own   powers
          in relation to
the laws passed

                              to control them

          the Choctaw and the Chickasaw tribes

                         have been made

                    to understand their true condition,

          submitting

                                        subsistence

a separate existence,
     inconveniences and vexations

          but   progress   for
                    powerful

          nations
     reconciles the mind to

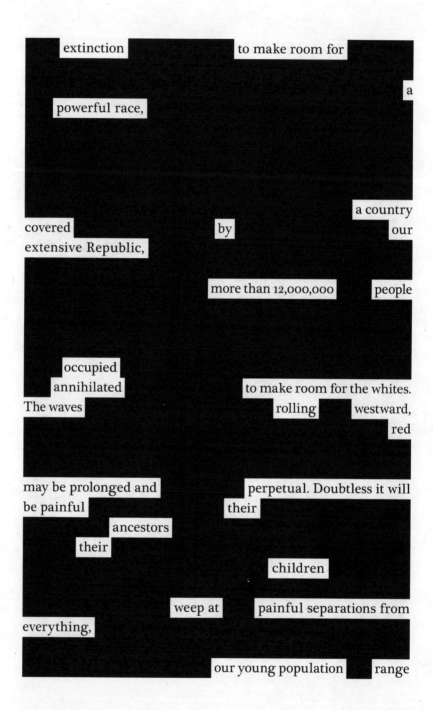

extinction   to make room for

                                                a

powerful race,

                                        a country
covered   by   our
extensive Republic,

                more than 12,000,000   people

        occupied
        annihilated   to make room for the whites.
The waves   rolling   westward,
                                                red

may be prolonged and   perpetual. Doubtless it will
be painful   their
        ancestors
    their

                        children

            weep at   painful separations from
everything,

                    our young population   range

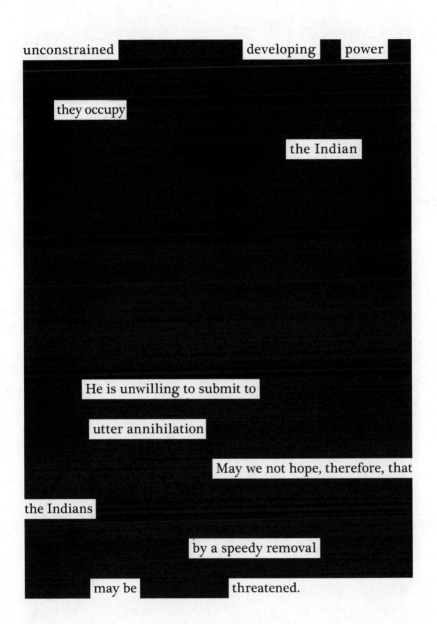

unconstrained   developing   power

they occupy

the Indian

He is unwilling to submit to

utter annihilation

May we not hope, therefore, that

the Indians

by a speedy removal

may be   threatened.

STILL THEY COME

My great-great-great-grandfather Henry Moon fought in Black Hawk's War, and though I don't know for which side, I can guess. Black Hawk and his people were killed because they wanted to live on land that belonged to them. Henry Moon supported Tippecanoe's grandson, who won his presidency. Old Tippecanoe, the president's grandfather, won his nickname by burning the town and winter food stores of Tecumseh's people. History calls it a battle.

History also says Tecumseh's people started it, which makes me think about the genealogy of beginnings, like seeds stored for a new season, but burned to ash, only good for painting stories. Henry Moon married a Mohican Indian, Abigail Abrams, a descendent of Sachem Benjamin Kokhkewenaunaunt. I wonder if his stories made him dream of an Indian princess? Or maybe he just wanted her land. The censuses won't tell me that. Henry and Abigail had a son who lived through the Civil War, but his mother died when he was nine. Because women weren't seen as newsworthy, I know even less about Abigail than Henry.

ACNESTIS 3

It's Thanksgiving when I pull out the plastic bins of photos. At the old house, they lived in the cubby under the stairs, in the same room with the terrible stuffed clown, Nicodemus, who my grandfather loved, and the desk where he hid his pocketknife and gold-plated yo-yo. But the house has been sold and foreclosed, gutted and rewired, rebuilt from the inside, so that I don't recognize the rooms anymore when my mother and I go on the open-house tour. The cubby is gone with the staircase, which has been shifted over a few feet. Something about beams and a bigger bathroom.

Now the pictures live in the twice-rescued buffet in my mother's apartment in a five-story cement building for senior citizens. When my mother was a child, my grandfather brought the buffet home from some curbside, braced what was broken, and finished it to a shine that hasn't faded in sixty years, thanks to my grandmother and then my mother, who also refused to let it go with the house, knowing how I liked to follow the scrollwork with my fingers, knowing that this, for some reason, was my link to home, the one thing I'd take with me, someday. Maybe because it used to live in the dining room, the center of holiday gatherings, every Christmas its top a snowy landscape of tiny plastic houses and fiberglass trees, the snowflakes we cut from coffee filters taped to the cream and gold wallpaper above.

Flipping through the old photos, I interrupt my mother's cooking to ask about this face and that. Some we know and other names are gone with my grandmother. The ones she knows I write on the back of the photos, careful notations for when I'm the last link between the past and whoever comes next.

I'm struck by one in particular, a handsome young man in black and white, plaid flannel, boots and gloves for winter. He's perched, casual and smiling, on the ice that piles up along Lake Michigan after a late storm pushes it to shore. Jaunty is the word, or maybe rakish, something of a '50s movie star. It's my great uncle Francis Cambray, my mother says, who died in World War II. From another drawer of the buffet, she pulls a black box a little bigger than her hand and opens it to the Purple Heart resting on gold velvet.

He was a paratrooper, but she doesn't really know what happened to him. I suppose the specifics didn't much matter when the telegram arrived. But now the specifics are easy enough to find in some online archive. It turns out he was dropped once at Normandy and lived to make it back to England. Then he was dropped a second time in Holland. The mission was to hold certain bridges and train trestles, so that the Allies would have a supply line across the southern part of the country. He died 4,000 miles from Lake Michigan, where the  picture was taken, but only 160 miles from Cambrai, France, where his ancestors were likely born. I hope he felt some sense of home, drifting down over a once-familiar landscape, or at least that the lake didn't feel so terribly far away.

DECEMBER

We buy and gift, go out in a fit
of tinsel and twinkle lights,

in other words, we end
with the best and worst in us.

Wrap up the year
in swaddling clothes,

and leave it
out in the cold.

ON A WIRE

The trees bend backwards, break
themselves bearing a foot of snow,
power lines sagging in their wake.

Northern trees muscle up or give up
through each weighted winter,
hunker down under blizzards.

It's the same for me. I thought
I bore each downfall with grace,
but nobody gave up their body like me.

A joy's worth of crows on a wire choruses,
Nobody, nobody, nobody. And I am left
echoing in their outro.

But then the moon, swinging easily
in the staff of skewed electric lines,
sings to me in C-major, and I dance

a different kind of giving up, her voice
descending into notes for which we
have no names—this one, the color

of a crow just at dusk on the last day
of the year, that one, my body, after
it's given in for the last time.

JANUARY

Every story begins
with one white page, but this

is a story about hindsight,
about the black marks we'll have

made after a long year of erasing,
when *confetti* autocorrects to *ash*.

ÔKUMAHAMUK WIYON

Ôkumaham wiyon konuk
yaqi uhkutuqash. Iyo, cáqan uyutáháwôk

nukôctomun yo kisk?
Patáhqáham acá kupat.

Katumuw pahkacihtôw áwaks.
Quhsháwôk nukôctomun yo kisk.

SNOW WADING MOON

The moon wades through snow
to its knees. Now, which emotion

will we hide today?
Thunder hunts the ice.

The year ends with fog.
We will hide fear today.

DIRECTIVE

I want to say I don't serve the dead,
but how not, in these dusty rooms
and among mounded graves?
At Aztalan, where settlers took

the Mississippian village for an Aztec temple,
I kneel at the top of the tallest built hill. I feel them
just over my shoulder, the ancestors. They smile,
and I am welcome here. They say, *It's okay.*

They say, *Just visit, like this, every now and then.*
We're well past the end of our story,
and no one can tell us again. They say,
Life was a good joke. Now turn

your pen to the children silenced
or missing or caged, and those
still to come, who might yet be
raised from the dead.

While I was finishing this book, over 1,000 graves, mostly
for children, were found at the sites of former Canadian
residential schools. I'm sure more will be found in both Canada
and the United States, and many more will never be found.
I have no words strong enough to speak to this loss.

For the survivors and for those who didn't,
Manto wuw kumihkunumuq wayômanicuk.
May the Creator hold you in the palm of his hand.

NOTES

TITLE: There are differing ideas on the etymology of the word "Wisconsin." However, one interpretation of the word is that it is an English and French appropriation of the Miami language word for the river now called the Wisconsin River. That word, "Meskonsing," refers to the river that "runs through a red place."

TRANSLATIONS: The Mohegan poems in this book were written using the *Modern Mohegan Dictionary* (2006), and the "Mohegan Phrase Book," both prepared by Stephanie Fielding. Some Mohegan poems use found language borrowed from sample translations.

WIYON (MOON) POEMS: The Mohegan year is based on the lunar cycle, beginning with Wiksapákat Wiyon, the Maple Sugar Moon, when the maple sap begins to flow in spring. Each moon has a story associated with it, from which each of the moon poems take their content. For example, whatever you are doing when you first hear the spring peepers during Kopayáhs Wiyon, you will continue doing until the last ice breaks the next year.

MOUND POEMS: Earthen mounds are abundant in Wisconsin and in many other states. They are indicative of complex cities and societies that interacted and traded across the continent. However, many have been partially or completely destroyed, like those that were dug up to provide a foundation for the Wisconsin State Capitol building.

"EFFIGY": Fidelia Fielding was the last fluent speaker of the Mohegan language, upon whose diaries the modern language is partially based.

"LUCY"/ "LUCY": Brothertown was first a town in Upstate New York, near the current hamlet of Deansboro, built on Oneida land, and established by peoples from several Christianized tribes who lived along the Atlantic coast during European contact (among them Mohegan, Pequot, Tunxis, Narraganset, Montauk, and Niantic). When the Brothertown people, now a unified group, migrated to Wisconsin, they established a new Brothertown on the eastern shore of Lake Winnebago.

"LOST": Article is from the *Green-Bay Intelligencer* archives, September 19, 1835.

"MUCÁQ"/"GONE": A red handprint and a red dress are contemporary symbols recognizing MMIWG2 (Missing and Murdered Indigenous Women, Girls, and Two-Spirit People). The movement seeks to bring recognition and justice to the epidemic of violence against Indigenous women, girls, and two-spirited people today and throughout history.

"PARRISH": The documents accompanying this poem are from Joseph Clark's "Account of a Journey to the Indian Country," written in 1797 and published in *Friends' Miscellany*, vol. 1, no. 8 (1831).

"MOHICAN" AND "THE WHITES OF NEW YORK": James Fenimore Cooper's popular book, *The Last of the Mohicans*, has done lasting damage to Indigenous peoples by portraying us as nearly extinct and destined to become so. Contrary to this misinformation, the Mohican people are alive and well.

"MOHICAN": The Carlisle Indian Industrial Boarding School was the model upon which the forced residential school system was built. Its founder, Richard Henry Pratt, believed that these schools should "Kill the Indian and save the man," meaning that they should strip away any Indigenous language, culture, or tradition in order to raise Indigenous children to Euro-American standards.

Residential schools in the United States and Canada were places of violence and trauma for generations of Indigenous children. My great-grandfather, William Moon, and his sisters all attended Carlisle before it was closed in 1918. It wasn't until 1978—just two years before I started school—that Indigenous parents were legally allowed to deny a child's placement in an off-reservation school.

"CEMETERY ETIQUETTE": The document accompanying this poem is part of an application for enrollment into the Eastern Cherokee tribe when the Guion Miller Rolls were being established. Original documents are held by the National Archives and Records Administration.

"THE WHITES OF NEW YORK": The epigraph for this poem comes from E. Pauline Johnson's poem, "The Cattle Thief," lines 49–52, originally published in her 1895 book, *The White Wampum.*

"MAN MOUNDS": The italicized sections of this poem are quoted from the "Draft environmental impact statement, disposal of Badger Army Ammunition Plant, Wisconsin" (2002), pages 3–74 and the "Badger Army Ammunition Plant" Wikipedia page.

"BETWEEN THE LINES": The source material is President Andrew Jackson's Message to Congress, "On Indian Removal," December 6, 1830; Records of the United State's Senate, 1789–1990; Record Group 46; Records of the United States Senate, 1789–1990; National Archives and Records Administration (NARA).

"STILL THEY COME": Articles are from the *Oshkosh Northwestern* newspaper archives, July 30, 1888 and December 2, 1889.

ACKNOWLEDGMENTS

No book is a solitary creation. Without the following people and organizations, this book could not exist in its current form. My greatest appreciation to everyone who made this work possible:

❀ The Brothertown Indian Nation

❀ Mike and Rose Pelky, for setting me on a genealogical research path, for doing so much of the work before I ever came along, and for sharing the stories.

❀ Aliki Barnstone, Joanna Hearne, Mark Palmer, and Alex Socarides, for being mentors and readers and for convincing me that I had something to say.

❀ Robert Tryon, for his invaluable help with Mohegan words and grammar.

❀ The Stockbridge-Munsee Band of Mohicans' Arvid E. Miller Memorial Library & Museum

❀ The Wisconsin Historical Society

❀ Dickinson University and the National Archives, for the Carlisle Indian School records.

❀ The University Archives at the University of Pennsylvania

❀ The Swarthmore College Archives

❀ Lana at Forest Home Cemetery in Marinette, Wisconsin

❀ And, of course, Rebecca Olander and the wonderful community at Perugia Press

ABOUT THE AUTHOR

Rebecca Pelky is a member of the Brothertown Indian Nation of Wisconsin and a native of Michigan's Upper Peninsula. She holds a PhD from the University of Missouri, an MFA from Northern Michigan University, and is an Assistant Professor of Film Studies at Clarkson University in Upstate New York. *Through a Red Place* is her second poetry collection; her first, *Horizon of the Dog Woman,* was published by Saint Julian Press in 2020.

ABOUT PERUGIA PRESS

Perugia Press publishes one collection of poetry each year, by a woman at the beginning of her publishing career. Our mission is to produce beautiful books that interest longtime readers of poetry and welcome those new to poetry. We also aim to celebrate and promote poetry whenever we can, and to keep the cultural discussion of poetry inclusive.

Also from Perugia Press:

* *Now in Color,* Jacqueline Balderrama
* *Hail and Farewell,* Abby E. Murray
* *Girldom,* Megan Peak
* *Starshine Road,* L. I. Henley
* *Brilliance, Spilling: Twenty Years of Perugia Press Poetry*
* *Guide to the Exhibit,* Lisa Allen Ortiz
* *Grayling,* Jenifer Browne Lawrence
* *Sweet Husk,* Corrie Williamson
* *Begin Empty-Handed,* Gail Martin
* *The Wishing Tomb,* Amanda Auchter
* *Gloss,* Ida Stewart
* *Each Crumbling House,* Melody S. Gee
* *How to Live on Bread and Music,* Jennifer K. Sweeney
* *Two Minutes of Light,* Nancy K. Pearson
* *Beg No Pardon,* Lynne Thompson
* *Lamb,* Frannie Lindsay
* *The Disappearing Letters,* Carol Edelstein
* *Kettle Bottom,* Diane Gilliam
* *Seamless,* Linda Tomol Pennisi
* *Red,* Melanie Braverman
* *A Wound On Stone,* Faye George
* *The Work of Hands,* Catherine Anderson
* *Reach,* Janet E. Aalfs
* *Impulse to Fly,* Almitra David
* *Finding the Bear,* Gail Thomas